Henry David Thoreau's
WALDEN

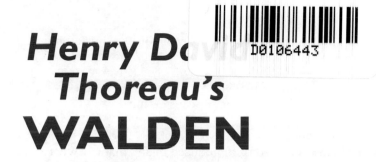

Charlotte Alexander

Department of English
New York University

BARNES
&NOBLE
BOOKS
NEW YORK

Copyright © 1997, 1965 by Simon & Schuster, Inc.

This edition published by Barnes & Noble, Inc.,
by arrangement with Macmillan Publishing USA,
a division of Simon & Schuster, Inc.

All rights reserved. No part of this book
may be used or reproduced in any manner whatsoever
without the written permission of the Publisher.

1997 Barnes & Noble Books

MACMILLAN is a registered trademark of Macmillan, Inc.
Monarch and colophons are trademarks of Simon & Schuster, Inc.,
registered in the U.S. Patent and Trademark Office.

Macmillan Publishing USA
A division of Simon & Schuster, Inc.
1633 Broadway
New York, NY 10019

ISBN 0-7607-0588-7

Text design by Tony Meisel

Printed and bound in the United States of America.

00 01 M 9 8 7 6 5 4 3 2

RRDC

CONTENTS

INTRODUCTION

Henry David Thoreau was born in Concord, Massachusetts, on July 12, 1817. After graduating from Harvard in 1837, he taught school, first at Concord, then in a private school opened with his brother John. He also began keeping his *Journal* upon graduation, and in 1837 made Ralph Waldo Emerson's acquaintance. During the period after college he began giving lectures and publishing essays, chiefly in the *Week* and the *Dial* (a Transcendental journal). He lived with the Emersons in 1841 and again after the Walden experience (1845–47), supervising the household in Emerson's frequent absence. From 1844 onward, making a living also included for him brief periods in his father's pencil-making factory and surveying. Also, from 1839 he was periodically making excursions on the Concord and Merrimack rivers and into the Maine woods and Cape Cod, the basis of later published writings. He went to Minnesota for his health in 1861 and died at Concord of tuberculosis on May 6, 1862.

HIGHLIGHTS OF THOREAU'S LIFE

From the brief biographical summary above emerge certain areas of some significance to Thoreau's work: the period right after college, including what appear to have been the two loves in his life, and his unending conflict about choosing a profession; his friendship with Ralph Waldo Emerson and his interest in Transcendentalism; and of course the excursions into "Nature" that produced his major works. It is generally assumed that he loved (but did not marry) two women in his life: one was Ellen Sewall, sister of his friend Edmund Sewall, to whom he proposed in the years after college and by whom he was rejected; the other was Lidian Emerson, wife of Ralph Waldo Emerson, a woman beautiful and severe, 15 years his senior, to whom he seems to have been devoted platonically for a number of years. Just out of college Thoreau was plagued with both choosing a profession suitable for a Harvard graduate and with simply earning a living. Although he never found himself able to fit into any of the categories assumed suitable for his education—divinity, law, academic teaching, lecturing, and research—and throughout his life elevated (as had Emerson in "The American Scholar") the "poet-philosopher" as his own ideal, he was annoyingly confronted from time to time with the problem of making a living: hence his periodic teaching and lecturing, his stays with the Emersons, during which time he was supposed to "make it" in the New York literary world (but did not), his frustrated periods of work in his father's pencil-making factory, surveying, and the day labor he did while at Walden and on other excursions. Thoreau's strong resistance to the drudgery necessary to make a go of it in the material world was of course linked to his belief that people should pursue their higher nature and discover their inner selves, probably through isolated meditation in a time of leisure; when forced into the hustling economic world he felt his life to be "prosaic, hard and coarse." In the essay "Life Without Principle," for example, he expressed his bitterness by asserting, "a man had better starve at once than lose his innocence in the process of getting his bread."

The influence of his Transcendentalist mentor Emerson on Thoreau was of course great, both through Emerson's writings such as "The American Scholar" (in which he idealizes the scholar's life of meditation and study) and "Nature" (in which we find the seed of many of Thoreau's ideas about Nature and humanity), and through his friendship with the Emersons. Yet their friendship proved a difficult one, in which Thoreau seems to have invoked an impossible ideal of communication on a "higher plane" between two philosophers. If Thoreau was idealistic, Emerson himself may have been slightly patronizing to the younger man: the inevitable result at any rate was antagonism, expressed for example in an excerpt from Thoreau's *Journal*—"Talked, or tried to talk, with R. W. E. Lost my time—nay, almost my identity. He, assuming a false opposition where there was no difference of opinion, talked to the wind—told me what I knew—and I lost my time trying to imagine myself somebody else to oppose him." His first stay with the Emersons, however (and tutoring Emerson's nephew on Staten Island), solidified his desires to withdraw from the civilized world for a while; he wrote in the *Journal*, "I don't want to feel as if my life were a sojourn any longer. The philosophy cannot be true which so paints it. It is time now that I begin to live." Hence the Walden experiment.

Friendship to Thoreau, though, was the highest Transcendental relation, without which Nature was not morally significant. Thus he went to Emerson (whose essay "Nature" had become the bible of the Transcendentalists), hoping that their relationship would be so ideal as to show the world "what men can build each other up to be, when both master and pupil work in love." (Basically, Transcendentalism explores the nature of reality, and there are several "philosophies" that fall into the general category of Transcendentalism; here we are concerned with an American Transcendentalism propounded chiefly in the ideas of Emerson, based on the search for reality through spiritual intuition.) Thoreau was able to respond intellectually to Emerson, however, in the sense that his own Transcendentalist ideas developed from those set forth in Emerson's "Nature." Briefly, those ideas, basic to the American Transcendentalist movement, are (1) conviction of knowledge beyond that given to us through the five senses; (2) spirit is supreme over matter; (3) Nature is to be enjoyed, even reverenced; and (4) the individual must set a high standard of personal conduct, which often includes an antimaterialistic view of the business world.

THOREAU'S WORKS

Thoreau's chief works are *A Week on the Concord and Merrimack Rivers* (1849), *Walden* (1854), *The Maine Woods* (1863), and certain essays such as "On the Duty of Civil Disobedience" (1849), "Slavery in Massachusetts" (1854), and "A Plea for John Brown" (1859). In addition there are his *Journal* accounts of various excursions, and letters and poems. Many of his essays were first presented as lectures or published in journals such as the *Dial* and *The Atlantic Monthly* and were collected posthumously. A comment can be added here about *A Week on the Concord and Merrimack Rivers,* published in 1849, two years after Thoreau emerged from Walden Woods; for he wrote these essays while at Walden and they can be said to encompass his spiritual history from 1839 to 1849 (just as *Walden* spans the spiritual struggles of 1845 to 1854). *A Week* and *Walden* may be regarded as companion volumes, chronicling his search for an organic life in Nature, from the easy, youthful communions to the intellectually harder-won communions of his adulthood. He himself financed the publication of the book and was disappointed in its lack of popular success. Just like *Walden, A Week* reveals as much of the poet-philosopher as it does of the traveler-sojourner.

THOREAU'S MAJOR THEMES AND IDEAS: SELF-AWARENESS

Thoreau's essential theme is life—but life lived when one is fully awake. As a Transcendentalist he was bound to explore the meaning of reality and seek his own inner self. This is why *Walden* is both an experience lived and an experience reflected on: while at Walden from 1845 to 1857 he of course kept his daily journal, but the book he published was the outgrowth of reflections on that past experiment and experience. *Walden* chronicles the spiritual self-searching of 1845 to 1854, which very importantly includes Thoreau's struggle to recapture afterward the purity and union with Nature that he felt in his simplified physical existence at Walden Pond. He did not look on his withdrawal to Walden in the search for self-realization as a permanently desirable isolation from society; but, as one of his critics puts it, "self-realization in Nature suffused him with love. Neither life nor love could be shared, he learned, until he had found his own center, the pride that rested on the security of his own self-reliance."

To find that center of the self, however, Thoreau believed that a "doctrine of simplicity" was desirable; the physically simplified life was the best means to self-emancipation. Through a kind of voluntary poverty, a materially simple existence, a direct line of communication between the inner self and Nature might be established. Thus he chose the pastoral life as the ideal milieu. In his *Journal* he wrote, "There are two kinds of simplicity, one that is akin to foolishness, the other to wisdom. The philosopher's style of living is only outwardly simple, but inwardly complex. The savage's style is both outwardly and inwardly simple." Thoreau is not, then, merely glorifying the life of the savage in his doctrine of simplicity (some of the American Transcendentalists, along with their counterparts among the English Romantic poets such as William Wordsworth and Samuel Taylor Coleridge, had elevated the primitive life as such, a tendency usually referred to as *primitivism*); a pastoral life is not necessarily a primitive life, as Thoreau was aware from his days at the pond and in Concord pastures when contrasted to life in the wilder Maine woods. Nor did he view the withdrawal to pastoral life at Walden Pond as escape but rather as discovery and strengthening of his higher nature, which he might then bring back into communion with society.

NATURE VERSUS "BARBARIC" CIVILIZATION

It is true, however, that the idealization of Nature was typical both of Transcendental thought in general and of Thoreau's personal philosophy. Nature administered to both physical and spiritual needs; there was a "correspondence" between humans and Nature—that is, every fact of Nature corresponded ideally with a fact of consciousness in the human mind. Furthermore, experience in Nature became idealized, "folded many times thick," as Thoreau described his experience at Walden as it had matured through his journal into the final version. Thoreau also described this correspondence between humanity and Nature in a poem titled "The Inward Morning":

Packed in my mind lie all the clothes
Which outward nature wears,
And in its fashion's hourly change
It all things else repairs.

In vain I look for change abroad,
And can no difference find,
Till some new ray of peace uncalled
Illumes my inmost mind.

This inward morning is the kind of wakeful awareness he stresses throughout *Walden*. It assesses the constant inspiration to be derived from Nature. What he was ultimately aiming at, of course, as philosopher and Transcendentalist, was union or a sense of complete oneness with Nature: in order to achieve this he attempted a disciplined, ascetic life—the idea of purity, purification of the channels of perception, often recurs in his writing—and he observes Nature closely, practically giving himself up to the life in Nature.

It is only natural that such a philosophy should emerge as antimaterialistic; added to this was Thoreau's personal distaste for materialistic striving, his refusal to subscribe to the prevailing Puritan work ethic, his dislike of organized authority (of church or state, for instance), and his disgust with the way civilized society seemingly obscured—even brutalized—people's inner, higher nature. This is why he said in *Walden* that "most men live lives of quiet desperation," trying to make a living and/or attempting to reach materialistic goals endorsed by the surrounding society. This is why he personally subscribed to the poet-philosopher's life of leisurely soul-study, in the face of strong opposition from those who believed in the maxim "work, for the night is coming." Thus he shows the "positive hindrances" of civilization by exposing in *Walden* such everyday matters as food, clothing, shelter, and furniture, as well as education, law, reform, to the test of fitness to a person's "inner necessities." The paradox of civilization, then, was that it actually "barbarized" people, since it drove them or caused them to drift farther away from awareness of their inner selves. By the same token, Thoreau contended that he had "civilized" himself by the experience of Walden, since he approached self-realization and oneness with Nature.

WALDEN (1854)

The germ of this volume is of course to be found in Thoreau's daily entries in his *Journal* during the two-year stay at Walden Pond, entries that attempt to capture the spontaneity of his life and experiences in Nature there. But, as pointed out, *Walden* is more than a mere record of the years 1845–47; it is that experience metaphorized by thought and revisions over the years until the book's appearance in 1854 (several editions of *Walden,* for example, distinguish ideas and passages altered or even added between the early and the later periods of its growth as a book). These revisions emphasize too that *Walden* is a more structurally unified work than a simple diary of events would be.

One large area of revisions and additions that made *Walden* a sophisticated, mature work was that of symbolism and imagery. Thoreau had seen that the narrative action might be condensed from two years into one and related to the four seasons. Such a structure enabled him to draw parallels with the seasons of life itself and to expand the symbolism of, say, spring into an elaborate metaphor of purification and rebirth. Also, within the episode of spring he chooses to focus on the thaw, which amounts to dropping one's shell or skin (the thick ice on the pond melts, as does the snow, flowing away to nourish new plants; flowers and trees and insects emerge from seed or shell), just as he emphasizes throughout the reptilian imagery to establish the idea of leaving an old, discontented, "barbarized" life and seeking a freshened, new existence. In his revisions he also elaborated on the day, which like the year had its seasons—especially morning, that most essential "waking" time: "Only that day dawns to which we are fully awake." The most insistent symbol in *Walden* is of course the pond, which represents that inner, deeper self that a person seeks to know.

"ON THE DUTY OF CIVIL DISOBEDIENCE" (1849)

The incident that precipitated this essay was Thoreau's arrest in July 1846 for refusal to pay his poll tax. Indeed, he had not paid tax since 1842, but on this occasion Sam Staples, the town jailer who would be required to pay Thoreau's tax if he did not, imprisoned him (he was at Walden at the time). He stayed in jail for only one night because friends paid his tax for him, as they did subsequently also. One night's stay in jail, though, however interesting, did not permit Thoreau to put the tax to a test. Furthermore, he had long been interested in the rights and responsibilities of the individual in relation to government (he considered this in *A Week on the Concord and Merrimack Rivers,* which he was at that time writing), and in 1848 he had lectured at the Concord Lyceum twice on civil disobedience. He makes clear his antislavery position in *Walden,* too (for his views on civil disobedience were grounded in his outrage at a government that permitted slavery and "overran unjustly" foreign countries such as Mexico), suggesting refusal to recognize the authority of "the State which buys and sells men, women, and children, like cattle at the door of its senate-house."

In this essay Thoreau is also invoking Transcendentalist principles of moral law, the idea that a person's conscience is his or her first guide; for the Transcendentalists felt that their materialistically geared society encouraged apathy, complacency, passivity, even moral cowardice in its citizens. In the place of these undesirable qualities Thoreau wished for individual citizens who would make up a "wise minority," offering against their government when they believed it to be wrong a passive resistance that was yet not so passive, since it was designed to clog the machinery and place obstacles in the path of the government. These ideas have of course come down to the present, from Mahatma Gandhi's philosophy through to the civil rights protests, in America.

WALDEN
CHAPTERS I–IV

CHAPTER I: ECONOMY

Thoreau begins the now-famous *Walden* very directly: "When I wrote the following pages, or rather the bulk of them, I lived alone, in the woods, a mile from any neighbor, in a house which I had built myself, on the shore of Walden Pond, in Concord, Massachusetts. . . . I should not obtrude my affairs so much on the notice of my readers if very particular inquiries had not been made by my townsmen concerning my mode of life. . . ."

COMMENT

Although such an opening—and the method of presentation throughout *Walden*—suggests the spontaneity of sheer reporting that Thoreau claims, this was not actually the case. *Walden* went through at least seven versions (revisions) before publication, and the bulk of the work that Thoreau may have written during his stay at the pond was either put down in the journal he had kept regularly since leaving Harvard, or was recorded in the first and roughest draft of *Walden*. It is important to establish at the outset that *Walden* is not merely a verbatim report of two years in the woods but is the creative expression of such an experience reflected on between 1845 and 1857.

The author apologizes for using the first person, "I," adding that "I should not talk so much about myself if there were any body else whom I knew as well. Unfortunately, I am confined to this theme by the narrowness of my experience. Moreover, I, on my side, require of every writer, first or last, a simple and sincere account of his own life, and not merely what he has heard of other men's lives." He further comments that "perhaps these pages are more particularly addressed to poor students."

COMMENT

Thoreau's remarks about use of first-person narrative are clearly exaggerated. First of all, he understood the value of the "I" in developing an atmosphere of authenticity and directness. Second, he is introducing the ironic tone he will sustain throughout, by stating that there was no one "else whom I knew so well," or admitting the "narrowness" of his experience (since, of course, he believed his experience at Walden to have been the most broadening one of his whole life). Furthermore, in referring to his prerequisite of "sincerity" in other writers as well as in himself, he is striking the chord of "nonconformity," as opposed to following the crowd ("merely what he has heard of other men's lives"): the idea of nonconformity is basic to all of Thoreau's thought. Finally, in mentioning that his pages are dedicated especially to "poor students," he is drawing on both biographical fact and cherished belief: he himself had been a poor student and indeed had been plagued all his life by the dulling necessity of making a living; yet his ideal for a life well lived—the life of a poet-philosopher—had remained in the face of all obstacles and criticism that of the "poor student," or, defined on a higher plane by Emerson in "The American Scholar," the man who simplifies his life in order that he may have energy and leisure to reflect "complexly" upon life. Thus the very title of the first chapter, "Economy," while certainly referring to the actual economies Thoreau practiced at Walden and at other times, is also ironic in its suggestion of spiritual economies forced on the author by the world outside, his temporary withdrawal to the woods in order to revitalize his spirit and realize his inner self.

Thereupon Thoreau launches his major attack upon his own American civilization—its materialistic values and its unthinking work ethic—preparing the ground for his own stripping down of such values through defining what are the actual

"necessaries" of life after all. Again he speaks with seeming
naiveté, saying it is necessary before proceeding to say a little
about the people of New England, whose young men, he
remarks, "might have seen with clearer eyes what field they
were called to labor in." That is, "Men labor under a mistake.
The better part of the man is soon ploughed into the soil for
compost. By a seeming fate, commonly called necessity, they
are employed, as it says in an old book, laying up treasures
which moth and rust will corrupt and thieves break through
and steal." Most men, to Thoreau, "are so occupied with the
factitious cares and superfluously coarse labors of life that its
finer fruits cannot be plucked by them." They are, in short,
burdened like "machines" with merely making a living.

COMMENT

The ideas of "vocation," the choice of it, and of making
a living, the necessity of it, were very dear to Thoreau.
From the time he graduated from Harvard in 1837 he
was subject to questions and criticism about his own
refusal to choose a vocation suitable for a Harvard man—
divinity, law, scholarly teaching, lecturing, or writing
would have been approved professions at the time. Similarly, since he lacked a background of wealth, he was
confronted from the first with making a living; but he
resented all money-making activities—from working in
his father's pencil-manufacturing concern, to supervising Emerson's household during his frequent absences,
to the occupation of surveyor—which inevitably, he
asserted, infringed on his individuality, sapped his
mental energy, and thus removed him farther from his
goal of realizing the inner self. When Thoreau claims
that "the mass of men lead lives of quiet desperation,"
then, he is also poignantly identifying himself with this
mass of men.

Thoreau therefore poses the important question as to what
are the real necessities of life, things essential to people any-

where, answering the question with a short list: food, shelter, clothing, fuel. These necessities he contrasts to the luxuries or comforts people think they must pursue but that are in reality hindrances to finding one's higher nature. Yet he sees it as practically inevitable, especially in urban life, for people to get caught in the trap of seeking after these frivolous luxuries after they have fulfilled the basic needs; furthermore, even in filling basic needs such as clothing and shelter people tend to follow each other like sheep, conforming to what is fashion or approved form rather than selecting what is functional or aesthetically pleasing.

Thoreau's solution to what he saw as the problem of modern civilization was to take to the woods, in order to learn more about the world and humanity and himself: "My purpose in going to Walden Pond was not to live cheaply nor to live dearly there, but to transact some private business with the fewest obstacles. . . ." His "private business" was to search his own soul, to find a self partly through the strict simplification of the externals of existence. His "capital" for the venture is quite in contrast to the fashion-conscious civilization he has left behind: his clothes are simple and sturdy; the hut he constructs is functional for all seasons (he describes in detail the building of this structure, 10 by 15 feet, with two large windows, a brick fireplace, a closet, one door, a shingled roof, which cost a total of $28.12½); his diet (also detailed) is unadorned, vegetarian yet tasty. On the building he did all the work himself (studying masonry, for example, to build the fireplace), financing it by a gardening project—especially beans—and also earning some money from surveying, carpentry, and day labor. (He seems to take special delight in the fact that his hut cost him less than a year's rent for a student at Cambridge College, remarking that "the student who wishes for a shelter can obtain one for a lifetime at an expense not greater than the rent which he now pays annually.") All Thoreau's earnings and expenditures, diet, and furnishings are here detailed.

Thus he discovered that he could support himself for a year on the earnings of six weeks, leaving himself free for study and reflection. Again he stresses the nonconformist motives, instead of motives of "laziness" (i.e., escapism), in selecting such a life, remarking, as was true, that he had once worked as a schoolteacher but disliked it because "my expenses were . . . out of proportion to my income, for I was obliged to dress and train, not to say think and believe, accordingly, and I lost my time into the bargain."

COMMENT

Here again what Thoreau really means by "expenses" is an expense of spirit, the frustration of conforming thoughts and beliefs as well as appearance to the customary forms. Thus imprisoned rather than free, he lost precious time that could have been devoted to probing the life of the spirit through communion with Nature since he has decided, partly through theory and partly through practice, that living close to Nature is living close to God and carries with it the approach to unity and purity of self.

CHAPTER II: WHERE I LIVED, AND WHAT I LIVED FOR

Thoreau begins, "At a certain season of our life we are accustomed to consider every spot as the possible site of a house. I have thus surveyed the country on every side within a dozen miles of where I live. In imagination I have bought all the farms in succession, for all were to be bought, and I knew their price." Thus he describes how he got to know each of the farmers and their lands, becoming known in the neighborhood as a "sort of real-estate broker." Thoreau in fact became interested in really buying one farm, the Hollowell farm, attracted by "its complete retirement . . . its bounding on the river . . . the gray color and ruinous state of the house and barn, and the dilapidated fences, which put such an interval between me and the last occupant . . . the hollow and lichen-covered apple trees . . . but above all, the recollection I had of it from my earliest voyages up the river, when the house was concealed behind a dense grove of red maples. . . ."

COMMENT

Thoreau continues by saying that he especially wanted to buy this farm to enjoy its "advantages" outlined above, before the owner Hollowell had completed his "improvements" such as repair, getting out rocks, cutting down the hollow trees; in short, the chief virtue of such a site for the author was its isolation, just as its principal "crop" for him would have been spiritual. But even this sort of purchase seemed too binding, for Thoreau closes by commenting, "But I would say to my fellows, once for all, As long as possible live free and uncommitted. It makes little difference whether you are committed to a farm or the county jail."

Thoreau stresses the unfinished and open quality of the cabin in which he took up his abode on Independence Day July 4, 1845: "Merely a defence against the rain," lacking a chimney or plastering, it had "a clean and airy look, especially in the morning." He is enchanted with its "auroral character," comparing it in remembrance to "a certain house on a mountain which I had visited a year before. This was an airy and unplastered cabin, fit to entertain a travelling god, and where a goddess might trail her garments." Most important to him is that the fresh air remains inside his house.

COMMENT

Thoreau is actually eulogizing the "auroral character" of his abode here and in the passages following, drawing a moral from Nature (as he was inclined to do from Transcendental principle and from personal belief). The freshness of the morning encourages awareness and simplicity and purity, all conducive to discovering the inner self, to feeling spiritual union with the whole cosmos. (Thoreau's idea of "simplicity," sometimes referred to as his "doctrine of simplicity," is that one's style of life must be simplified in order that the spirit be freed to philosophize and find itself. In other words, simplicity to Thoreau did not suggest a bovine character of mental life; rather, he felt that a simple, peaceful pastoral setting was the ideal cradle for birth of complex thoughts.) Thus he asserts, "Every morning was a cheerful invitation to make my life of equal simplicity, and I may say innocence, with Nature herself. . . . Morning brings back the heroic ages. . . . The morning, which is the most memorable season of the day, is the awakening hour. Then there is least somnolence in us; and for an hour, at least, some part of us awakes which slumbers all the rest of the day and night." It is plain that "morning" takes on symbolic, creative significance for him, suggestive of rebirth: "Poetry and art, and the fairest and most memorable of the actions of men, date from such an hour." His message, therefore, spoken alike to himself and his audience, is that "we must learn to reawaken and keep ourselves awake, not by mechanical aids, but by an infinite expectation of the dawn, which does not forsake us in our soundest sleep."

Again Thoreau returns to the "business" he had to transact at Walden (mentioned in "Economy") in stating, "I went to the woods because I wished to live deliberately, to front only the essential facts of life, and see if I could not learn what it had to teach, and not, when I came to die, discover that I had not lived. I did not wish to live what was not life, living is so dear; nor did I wish to practise resignation, unless it was quite necessary. I wanted to live deep and suck out all the marrow of life . . . to drive life into a corner, and reduce it to its lowest terms, and, if it proved to be mean, why then to get the whole and genuine meanness of it, and publish its meanness to the world; or if it were sublime, to know it by experience, and be able to give a true account of it in my next excursion. For most men, it appears to me, are in a strange uncertainty about it, whether it is of the devil or of God. . . ."

COMMENT

This passage contains the core of Thoreau's intent and belief, both in living and writing *Walden*. All the thoughts contained here are elaborated on in the following chapters. It seems clear from this passage that Thoreau's withdrawal from civilized urban society was, even in his mind, a temporary and somewhat artificial one, rather than escapism, as some critics have supposed; for him it had become a "necessity" to front the essentials of life, to arrange his circumstances so that he could do this—the earnestness and pathos of this desire are seen in "I did not wish to live what was not life, living is so dear." It is a rather natural confrontation for a thoughtful young man of 28.

By "resignation" Thoreau means giving oneself up to the humdrum, dulling existence of merely acquiring material possessions, of only earning a living. Note that he adds, "unless it was quite necessary." In truth, Thoreau, like most men, was compelled frequently throughout his life both before and after Walden to resign himself to earning his bread. Knowledge of this fact, knowledge of what seems here to be his foreshadowing awareness and fear of it, is what indeed makes *Walden* more poignant than an unreflecting autobiographical report of a two-year sojourn in the woods could ever be.

In the period after 1845–47, therefore, Thoreau felt himself sometimes trapped in just the way he cautions us not to allow ourselves to be, by civilized society, so that the record of his experience that evolved during these years and was finally presented in 1854 contains also his depressions and his struggle to regain the spiritual exaltation he felt at Walden.

CHAPTER III: READING

Thoreau begins by asserting: "With a little more deliberation in the choice of their pursuits, all men would perhaps become essentially students and observers, for certainly their nature and destiny are interesting to all alike. In accumulating property for ourselves or our posterity, in founding a family or a state, or acquiring fame even, we are mortal; but in dealing with truth we are immortal, and need fear no change nor accident." His own choice of residence, therefore, is more favorable to reading and meditation than a university; while he has access to fewer books, and does not have full time at present to devote to reading (since he has had his house to finish and his beans to hoe), the time he spends with these books is most fruitful.

Thoreau praises the ancient "heroic" books, such as those of Homer, Virgil, and Aeschylus, as ideal reading material inasmuch as we may "in some measure emulate their heroes, and consecrate morning hours to their pages." (We recall that to the author the morning hours are the most precious, because it is then he feels most mentally alert.) He further approves reading these classics in the original languages: "It is worth the expense of youthful days and costly hours, if you learn only some words of an ancient language. . . ." The reader must, of course, bring to a book the same spirit of deliberation and effort that the author expended in writing it. Thoreau also cites the "scriptures of the nation"—the Bible, the *Vedas* and *Zendavestas* of the Hindus, other sacred books, Dante, and Shakespeare—as worthwhile reading.

He laments the fact, however, that great books are read by so few, asking for example, "What does our Concord culture amount to?" His main point here is that "even the college-bred and so-called liberally educated men here and elsewhere have really little or no acquaintance with the English classics." Too many men regard reading as a practical convenience, using this faculty as they have developed it merely for daily newspaper perusal or for "easy reading." Thoreau cites an amusing anecdote: "Most men are satisfied if they read or hear read, and perchance have been convinced by the wisdom of one good book, the Bible, and for the rest of their lives vegetate and dissipate their faculties in what is called easy reading. There is a work in several volumes in our Circulating Library entitled Little Reading, which I thought referred to a town of that name which I had not been to."

COMMENT

It should be noted that in suggesting that with more deliberate choice of profession "all men would perhaps become essentially students and observers," Thoreau is once again (as he does throughout) elevating the position of the "scholar" in society, the person who chooses a life of reading and meditation; he wishes to be for the most part a poet-philosopher. Thoreau had been influenced in this view by Emerson and his famous essay "The American Scholar," first presented before Thoreau's graduating class of Harvard and addressed to young men like Thoreau: Emerson too urged the casting aside of professions of business—devotion to the acquisition of material items, that is—in favor of a scholarly life. The scholar, Emerson said on another occasion, "is the favorite of Heaven and earth, the excellency of his country, the happiest of men. . . . His successes are occasions of the purest joy to all men."

Also, this chapter is an extension of a previous article in which Thoreau had discussed literature and "scripture." Literature was one way of borrowing from the past, a source of inspiration for present living. It was his intention to combine such inspiration from the past and the great with his present experiment in living: from all these sources assimilated into his consciousness would come, he believed, the divine revelation of living experience. Nature, however, was still the main avenue to the inner life; and his next chapter continues the "experiment" by discussing "Sounds."

Thoreau closes the chapter by specifically criticizing New England for its hypocrisy in the face of cultural expansion. "We boast that we belong to the nineteenth century and are making the most rapid strides of any nation. But consider how little this village does for its own culture." Concord is his example. He asserts that there are not decent libraries or secondary and adult schools in all of New England, since the community lavishes expenditure on "almost any article of bodily aliment or ailment than on our mental aliment." On the contrary, a rich country should be the first to patronize the fine arts. Accusing New England of provincialism, then, he issues a challenge: "To act collectively is according to the spirit of our institutions; and I am confident that, as our circumstances are more flourishing, our means are greater than the nobleman's. New England can hire all the wise men in the world to come and teach her, and board them round the while, and not be provincial at all. That is the *uncommon* school we want. Instead of noblemen, let us have noble villages of men. If it is necessary, omit one bridge over the river, go round a little there, and throw one arch at least over the darker gulf of ignorance which surrounds us."

COMMENT

Even back in his college days Thoreau had written urging that the state institute compulsory public education. He always subscribed to legislation helpful to the general public welfare. In the tone of the above passage, however, there is also a hint of the individualist who would refuse to pay his poll tax on the principle that his community's government was not as good as it could be: this incident is described and reflected on in his essay "On the Duty of Civil Disobedience."

CHAPTER IV: SOUNDS

Just as the chapter "Reading" describes the discipline of using the past for inspiration, so "Sounds" suggests the discipline of "reading" Nature. Thoreau's sense of hearing seems to have been acute, providing him with many insights into the sounds of living Nature. He asks: "Will you be a reader, a student merely, or a seer? Read your fate, see what is before you, and walk on into futurity." Although the first summer was partly occupied with manual work that kept him from reading much, there were also times when he "could not afford to sacrifice the bloom of the present moment to any work, whether of the head or hands." Thus he would sometimes sit in his sunny doorway all the morning, listening and thinking, contemplating the forest, birds, animals, the distant highway. He describes some of the local wildlife; then, upon hearing a far-off train whistle, he launches into a digression on the railroad and the changes it has brought to life and to commerce, acknowledging that commercial life has its advantages as well as its drawbacks. He goes on to speak of other sounds that are a part of his daily life—church bells, the distant lowing of a cow, the whippoorwills chanting, and, amusingly, owls: "I rejoice that there are owls. Let them do the idiotic and maniacal hooting for men. It is a sound admirably suited to swamps and twilight woods which no day illustrates, suggesting a vast and undeveloped nature which men have not recognized. They represent the stark twilight and unsatisfied thoughts which all have."

COMMENT

This chapter is the clearest indication so far of Thoreau's conviction that an acute awareness of the motions of Nature, meditated upon, was the entrance to a spiritual world linked to the world of Nature. The gateway to the life of the spirit—the inner life he sought—was through blending oneself into Nature as far as possible.

WALDEN
CHAPTERS V–X

CHAPTER V: SOLITUDE

This chapter continues the idea of communion with nature, beginning with "this is a delicious evening, when the whole body is one sense, and imbibes delight through every pore. I go and come with a strange liberty in Nature, a part of herself." It is an unusually "congenial" evening, with bullfrogs trumping, sounds of whippoorwills, a cool breeze. He returns home to find that visitors have left calling cards—flowers, evergreen, a name penciled on a yellow walnut leaf or a chip. He remarks on the solitude of his place, with the nearest neighbor a mile distant, with very few travelers stopping to disturb "the black kernel of the night." He comments that perhaps "men are generally still a little afraid of the dark, though the witches are all hung, and Christianity and candles have been introduced." At the same time, Thoreau insists that his solitude was not morbid or melancholy, for "there can be no very black melancholy to him who lives in the midst of Nature and has his senses still." He sees even the rain as a source of cheer—nourishment for his beans—rather than a dreary occasion, saying that some of his pleasantest hours were spent during the long rainstorms of the spring or the fall, confined as he was to his house, "soothed by their ceaseless roar and pelting."

When people ask him if he is lonesome where he lives, therefore, he feels like replying, "This whole earth which we inhabit is but a point in space. How far apart, think you, dwell the two most distant inhabitants of yonder star, the breadth of whose disk cannot be appreciated by our instruments? Why should I feel lonely? Is not our planet in the Milky Way? This which you put seems to me not to be the most important question. What sort of space is that which separates a man from his fellows and makes him solitary? I have found that no exertion of the legs can bring two minds much nearer to one another."

COMMENT

This was indeed a "most important question" to Thoreau, the question of communication—even communion, according to his ideal of friendship—between people. Friendship, he believed, should involve just this sort of exchange of thoughts, ideas, philosophy between people who sought their own higher nature, who were aware of the inner life. It was a very high standard for human relations that Thoreau set for himself and others, and his biographers generally picture him as inclined toward few rather than many close friendships. Even the exalted Emerson could not measure up to Thoreau's ideal for friendship, for he complained on more than one occasion of not being able to reach that higher plateau of communication with Emerson, his mentor.

Furthermore, Thoreau continues, there is a kind of aloneness that is always with us, in the sense that we sometimes step outside our own thoughts or actions and become spectators: "By a conscious effort of the mind we can stand aloof from actions and their consequences . . . I only know myself as a human entity; the scene, so to speak, of thoughts and affections; and am sensible of a certain doubleness by which I can stand as remote from myself as from another. However intense my experience, I am conscious of the presence and criticism of a part of me, which, as it were, is not a part of me, but spectator, sharing no experience, but taking note of it." Thus Thoreau finds it "wholesome to be alone the greater part of the time."

He even insists that we often see our close associates too often, making society "cheap" and "not having had time to acquire any new value for each other." In addition, when men do their daily work, they are in a sense alone.

He closes the chapter by evoking again this kindredness that he feels with Nature. "I have a great deal of company in my house; especially in the morning," he says, and cites the company of the dandelion, the loon, the sun. "I am no more lonely than the Mill Brook, or a weathercock, or the north star, or the south wind, or an April shower, or a January thaw, or the first spider in a new house." Thus he makes it clear that he thinks of Nature as almost "animate," its fellows as much companions as human beings.

CHAPTER VI: VISITORS

Perhaps desiring to qualify his remarks on solitude and companionship, Thoreau asserts, "I think that I love society as much as most, and am ready enough to fasten myself like a bloodsucker for the time to any full-blooded man that comes in my way. I am naturally no hermit, but might possibly sit out the sturdiest frequenter of the bar-room, if my business called me thither." He describes his ways of entertaining company at Walden. "I had three chairs in my house; one for solitude, two for friendship, three for society. When visitors came in larger and unexpected numbers there was but the third chair for them all, but they generally economized the room by standing up." He observes that our houses are in general too large for us, that he was able to entertain 25 or 30 people at a time in his little house without a crowded feeling.

He admits however that "big thoughts" need space. "One inconvenience I sometimes experienced in so small a house, the difficulty of getting to a sufficient distance from my guest when we began to utter the big thoughts in big words. You want room for your thoughts to get into sailing trim and run a course or two before they make their port. . . . If we are merely loquacious and loud talkers, then we can afford to stand very near together, cheek by jowl, and feel each other's breath; but if we speak reservedly and thoughtfully, we want to be farther apart, that all animal heat and moisture may have a chance to evaporate." He concedes then that his best room, his "withdrawing room, always ready for company, on whose carpet the sun rarely fell, was the pine wood behind my house."

When only one guest came, he shared a simple meal; more company brought no mention of food, and Thoreau states (in the same gently ironic tone that pervades this chapter, resulting in a certain charm of written style that is characteristic of Thoreau) that his reputation as a host never suffered from such "omissions." He relates a story about the visit of Winslow, governor of the Plymouth Colony, to the village of Chief Massassoit to illustrate this view of entertaining. He had, in fact, more visitors at Walden than during any other period in his life (a bit misleading, since he adds, "I mean that I had some"); furthermore, few came on trivial business. One of Thoreau's favorite visitors was a Canadian wood chopper and post maker: Thoreau calls him a "true Homeric or Paphlagonian man" who has heard of Homer, reads books on rainy days, but is not corrupted by civilization. He has a "slumbering" mind, its seeds not yet awakened to discipline of expression. "To him Homer was a great writer, though what his writing was about he did not know. A more simple and natural man it would be hard to find. Vice and disease, which cast such a sombre moral hue over the world, seemed to have hardly any existence for him. . . . He interested me because he was so quiet and solitary and so happy withal; a well of good humor and contentment which overflowed at his eyes. His mirth was without alloy. . . . In him the animal man chiefly was developed. In physical endurance and contentment he was cousin to the pine and the rock. . . . But the intellectual and what is called spiritual man in him were slumbering as in an infant." This man refused to play a part in the world; people who got to know him simply watch him unfold. He was so humble and simple that "humility was no distinct quality in him." He did not wish to change the world, for he truly liked it as it was (and as he knew it). However, "There was a certain positive originality, however slight, to be detected in him, and I occasionally observed that he was thinking for himself and expressing his own opinion, a phenomenon so rare that I would any day walk ten miles to observe it."

COMMENT

It is possible that, as he says, Thoreau did wonder whether the wood chopper was "wise as Shakespeare or as simply ignorant as a child." He seems to be exploring his own views here on what can be called a "primitive" type of person. He stresses and admires the Canadian's great simplicity and lack of guile; at the same time he believes—rather, he wants to believe—that the man is possessed of latent intellectual and spiritual powers, since these elements would make him fully kindred to Thoreau. We can make a distinction here between the terms *primitive* and *pastoral,* though: primitive, or *primitivism* (a term that is applied by some critics, rejected by others, with respect to Thoreau), refers to a person living in a practically animal or savage state, without any overlay of outside civilization, in crude physical environs, and with his or her mental life at least undetermined; pastoral, however (and pastoralism has also been applied to Thoreau), suggests rural life (perhaps also farming) lived by people with some experience of civilization who choose the pastoral life for what it has to offer them, in simplicity, in potential for meditation and spiritual growth. It is probably the pastoral rather than the strictly primitive life that Thoreau elevates in *Walden* and in his admiration of the wood chopper.

His other guests included travelers, beggars, even a simple-minded pauper, whose "half wit" causes him to observe wryly that "with respect to wit, I learned that there was not much difference between the half and the whole." The half-wit presented Thoreau "a metaphysical puzzle. . . . I have rarely met a fellow-man on such promising ground,—it was so simple and sincere and so true all that he said." (Here again we might infer that Thoreau's own powers of intellect and his obsessive urge to simplicity may be overestimating the "truth" of the half-wit's words.) Runaway slaves too stopped rather frequently at Thoreau's place; he always helped them northward (later in life Thoreau became involved with the abolitionist cause). There were also women and young children from the towns, walking for pleasure in the woods, and a lot of workingmen on their days off—"honest pilgrims" seeking the woods for "freedom's sake."

CHAPTER VII: THE BEAN-FIELD

Thoreau's one concentrated labor of the summer was growing beans, of which he had planted two and a half acres. He cannot quite explain to himself what seems to be, as they progress, almost the spiritual necessity of growing them. "What was the meaning of this so steady and self-respecting, this small Herculean labor, I knew not. I came to love my rows, my beans, though so many more than I wanted. They attached me to the earth, and so I got strength. . . . What shall I learn of beans or beans of me? I cherish them, I hoe them, early and late I have an eye to them, and this is my day's work." He pauses to reflect that he was brought to this very place, this very pond, when he was but four years old, and that "to-night my flute has waked the echoes over that very water." Then he continues to describe in some detail what he learned of bean husbandry, how he uncovered arrowheads and other relics of the ancient Indian cultivators of that same ground where his beans were growing. Sometimes on "gala days" the towns would fire guns, causing him to reflect on the preservation of the "liberties of Massachusetts" and of the nation, and to return to his labor "cheerfully with a calm trust in the future."

Thoreau itemizes (with a quaint grace) the commercial usefulness of his beans and other crops in terms of "outgoes" ($14.72½) and "income" ($23.44), with a profit of $8.71½. He is proud of his actual success at farming, but it is clear that his profit therein has been chiefly spiritual, on which he comments at length, observing first that "those summer days which some of my contemporaries devoted to the fine arts in Boston or Rome, and others to contemplation in India, and others to trade in London or New York, I thus, with the other farmers of New England, devoted to husbandry." But his "further experience" was that he said to himself, "I will not plant beans and corn with so much industry another summer, but such seeds, if the seed is not lost, as sincerity, truth, simplicity, faith, innocence, and the like, and see if they will not grow in this soil, even with less toil and manurance, and sustain me, for surely it has not been exhausted for these crops."

COMMENT

The symbolism of roots and seeds in Nature and in his own nature figures largely here in Thoreau's thinking. He loved the beans because they attached him to the earth; in other words, they increased his sense of kindredness with Nature. The actual seeds become further seeds of virtue in his mind because they symbolize the potential harvest of spending these months in solitude and constant communion with Nature. He realizes, however, that the virtues he aspires to, the exalted inner life, will be more difficult to produce than the actual bean crop.

He closes, not surprisingly, by linking farming—husbandry—to the past, claiming that "ancient poetry and mythology suggest, at least, that husbandry was once a sacred art; but it is pursued with irreverent haste and heedlessness by us, our object being to have large farms and large crops merely. We have no festival, nor procession, nor ceremony. . . ." Returning to his bean crop, he attempts to grasp the greater implications: "This broad field which I have looked at so long looks not to me as the principal cultivator, but away from me to influences more genial to it, which water and make it green. These beans have results which are not harvested by me."

COMMENT

Thoreau here is elevating the profession of farming, especially by citing ancient authority that husbandry was formerly considered a sacred art. This is why he speaks of the "true husbandman" devoted more to the studied cultivation than the produce of his fields, as opposed to the modern farmer who is as obsessed with material gain as his businessman counterpart in the towns. This is again Thoreau's emphasis on the pastoral way of life as most conducive to self-realization, and to communion with Nature so vital to that inner spiritual discovery: for Thoreau, Nature and the Godlike in humanity are forever intermingled.

CHAPTER VIII: THE VILLAGE

Sometimes after hoeing or studying (reading and writing) in the morning Thoreau would bathe himself in the pond, then walk to the village. He says, "As I walked in the woods to see the birds and squirrels, so I walked in the village to see the men and boys. . . ." He also went to hear some of the gossip that went on "incessantly" there. Yet after visiting with people whose company he cared about (avoiding the gossipers as much as possible, as well as the signs of material worlds—the dry goods store, the tavern, the tailor—hung along the streets to allure him and others), he always looked forward to returning to his haven. "It was very pleasant, when I staid late in town, to launch myself into the night, especially if it was dark and tempestuous, and set sail from some bright village parlor or lecture room, with a bag of rye or Indian meal upon my shoulder, for my snug harbor in the woods. . . ." He comments that he could find his way so well in the dark, that he often would direct visitors in the woods who had stayed until dark and were unable to find their way.

COMMENT

Here again Thoreau chooses to emphasize the symbolic significance of being lost in the woods. "Every man has to learn the points of compass again as often as he awakes, whether from sleep or any abstraction. Not till we are lost, in other words, not till we have lost the world, do we begin to find ourselves, and realize where we are and the infinite extent of our relations." His idea of course is that he himself had to lose the civilized world in withdrawal to Walden before he could find himself, his inner spiritual self. There is a hint here too of the symbolic meaning of the pond, representing that inner self he went in search of—for he always returns to the pond, to live, to meditate, suggesting that for inner peace, a person must always lose the world to some extent and turn inward to his or her own personal resources.

He relates in this chapter how, on going to the village to pick up a shoe at the cobbler's shop one afternoon in the summer of 1845, he was arrested and kept in jail overnight, because he "did not pay a tax to, or recognize the authority of, the state which buys and sells men, women, and children, like cattle at the door of its senate-house." (He is protesting the institution of human slavery, existing then within the bounds of his state of Massachusetts.) He concludes that "wherever a man goes, men will pursue and paw him with their dirty institutions, and if they can, constrain him to belong to their desperate odd-fellow society." (His protest toward this perceived situation was formalized in the famous essay "On the Duty of Civil Disobedience," first published in 1849; this is why he says, "as I have related elsewhere," since the treatise was published before *Walden* was.)

Thoreau notes in fact that he has never been molested by anyone except the government, that he "had no lock nor bolt but for the desk which held my papers, not even a nail to put over my latch or windows." He never locked his doors, yet his house was respected by private individuals. He closes with advice to those who govern to shun punishments and love virtue; then the people will be virtuous. "The virtues of a superior man are like the wind; the virtues of a common man are like the grass; the grass, when the wind passes over it, bends."

CHAPTER IX: THE PONDS

When he was not hoeing or studying, Thoreau found other diversions such as picking delicious huckleberries, joining a silent fisherman on the pond, or often on a late, warm evening, sitting in his boat playing the flute. Sometimes, too, having returned from the village and visiting, he would fish in the moonlight for the next day's meal, "serenaded" by owls and foxes or the "creaking note" of some bird. His real intent in this chapter, however, is to describe the scenery of Walden and the other ponds around. "The scenery of Walden is on a humble scale, and, though very beautiful, does not approach to grandeur. . . . Yet this pond is so remarkable for its depth and purity as to merit a particular description." Thereupon he details the "deep green well" that is Walden, although he adds, as to its color, that "lying between the earth and the heavens, it partakes of the color of both." The water is so transparent that you can see the bottom at 25 or 30 feet, as well as schools of perch and shiners as you paddle over it. (He relates the incident of losing his axe through an ice hole in winter; perceiving it at the bottom some 25 feet under, he was able to retrieve it.) Walden's shore is made up of smooth rounded white stones like paving stones, except for a few short sandy beaches. The pond rises and falls, but in a pattern that he cannot determine, although he notes that its sister ponds, Flints' and White, respond similarly.

There are other ponds in the vicinity: Flints', known otherwise as Sandy Pond, covers 197 acres; there is also Goose Pond, Fair Haven Pond, and White Pond, which he considers to be the most beautiful, although he loves Walden best. He describes each pond in some detail and speaks of them as lakes, "the landscape's most beautiful and expressive feature." But especially he describes how Walden served him well in all seasons, providing his drinking water as well as fish, and attracting to it other forms of wildlife. He is concerned to picture Walden's changing, seasonal beauty, concluding, "Nevertheless, of all the characters I have known, perhaps Walden wears best, and best preserves its purity. Many men have been likened to it, but few deserve that honor."

COMMENT

Critics tend to agree that the seasons of Walden pond are to be likened to the seasons of Thoreau's spiritual life; and it does seem to emerge especially in this chapter that Thoreau thought of the pond as his essential self (and the shore, perhaps, as his actual outer self). It might follow, therefore, that through "discipline" such as cultivating beans (whose seeds represent "virtues," we recall, and whose roots attach him to the earth), Thoreau expects to make this actual outer self (the shore) more satisfying, more in tune with the pristine inner self of the pond.

CHAPTER X: BAKER FARM

This chapter contains an account of his journeying to Fair Haven for an afternoon of fishing, and being forced by a sudden rainstorm to take refuge at Baker Farm, a farm inhabited and worked by John Field, an Irish laboring man, with his wife and several children. He sees Field as "an honest, hard-working, but shiftless man plainly," whose wife struggles to cook "successive dinners" on an ancient stove. Talking to Field "as if he were a philosopher, or desired to be one," Thoreau tries to convert him to his own simplified way of life, but without success, since the laborer, though poor, is not inclined to give up what he has already grubbed out of the ground. They go fishing together, and Field's luck remains "bad" while Thoreau catches a fair string of fish. Thoreau laments the crudeness and narrowness of a life such as John Field's, reflecting how "men come tamely home at night only from the next field or street, where their household echoes haunt, and their life pines because it breathes its own breath over again; their shadows morning and evening reach farther than their daily steps. We should come home from far, from adventures, and perils, and discoveries every day, with new experience and character." But this is a life of the spirit and the mind that the Thoreaus, not the John Fields, aspire to and sometimes reach. John Field, Thoreau reluctantly concludes, was born to be poor physically and spiritually.

WALDEN
CHAPTERS XI–XVIII

CHAPTER XI: HIGHER LAWS

This chapter treats sensuality, the animal instinct in men. Thoreau's thoughts have been turned down these paths by glimpsing a woodchuck running across his path as he came home at night from fishing. He reflects that he "felt a strange thrill of savage delight, and was strongly tempted to seize and devour him raw; not that I was hungry then, except for that wildness which he represented." He goes on to observe that he finds dual urges within himself and is not distressed by them. "I found in myself, and still find, an instinct toward a higher, or, as it is named, spiritual life, as do most men, and another toward a primitive rank and savage one, and I reverence them both. I love the wild not less than the good." These urges may go back to his hunting episodes in childhood, he says. From a discussion of fishing and studying fowls, he goes on to explain his own vegetarian tastes, claiming that bread or potatoes do as well as meat, and with less uncleanness, his chief objection to animal foods. Furthermore, he believes that vegetarianism encourages the higher nature in man, "that every man who has ever been earnest to preserve his higher or poetic faculties in the best condition has been particularly inclined to abstain from animal food, and from much food of any kind." And indeed, his own tastes are abstemious; he believes that "water is the only drink for a wise man; wine is not so noble a liquor; and think of dashing the hopes of a morning with a cup of warm coffee, or of an evening with a dish of tea!"

Yet the real issue with Thoreau seems to be his conviction of man's sensual nature, which must be controlled. "Our whole life is startlingly moral. There is never an instant's truce between virtue and vice. Goodness is the only investment that never fails." Thus it may be that he mistrusts the sensualities of food and drink and even, sometimes, music. "We are conscious of an animal in us, which awakens in proportion as our higher nature slumbers. It is reptile and sensual, and perhaps cannot be wholly expelled; like the worms which, even in life and health, occupy our bodies. Possibly we may withdraw from it, but never change its nature." "Temperance and purity," then, would be his goals, even if unattainable. And Thoreau insists that "the spirit can for the time pervade and control every member and function of the body, and transmute what in form is the grossest sensuality into purity and devotion. The generative energy, which, when we are loose, dissipates and makes us unclean, when we are continent invigorates and inspires us. Chastity is the flowering of man; and what are called Genius, Heroism, Holiness, and the like, are but various fruits which succeed it. Man flows at once to God when the channel of purity is open."

COMMENT

The key word here is perhaps *purity*, whether Thoreau speaks in terms of chastity, temperance, sloth: the more he is able to simplify his life, the more is the channel to godliness, to a life of the spirit, likely to be opened.

Thoreau here sees all sensuality as the same, "whether a man eat, drink, cohabit, sleep sensually. They are but one appetite." He admits that chastity is difficult to define, though. He affirms that "from exertion come wisdom and purity; from sloth ignorance and sensuality." Thus in a student sensuality might take the form, according to Thoreau, of a lazy mind, of lack of industry. We know chastity best, then, by its opposites. To avoid uncleanness and sins "work earnestly, though it be at cleaning a stable." He believes that silence, however, on the subject of something like the body's functions, is just another form of impurity. "We are so degraded that we cannot speak simply of the necessary functions of human nature. In earlier ages, in some countries, every function was reverently spoken of and regulated by law. Nothing was too trivial for the Hindoo lawgiver, however offensive it may be to modern taste. He teaches how to eat, drink, cohabit, void excrement and urine, and the like, elevating what is mean, and does not falsely excuse himself by calling these things trifles." (As will be seen, Thoreau exhibits throughout the influence of Oriental thought and philosophy.) Everyone builds his or her own temple which is the body, Thoreau says, according to the gods he or she worships. "We are all sculptors and painters, and our material is our own flesh and blood and bones. Any nobleness begins at once to refine a man's features, any meanness or sensuality to imbrute them."

CHAPTER XII: BRUTE NEIGHBORS

This chapter opens with a dialogue between a poet and a hermit, the poet a companion who came through the village to Thoreau's hut to fish with him. After reflecting momentarily on the great concepts that were in his mind before the poet's arrival and trying to recapture the thoughts, he agrees to go fishing.

COMMENT

The "poet" apparently was William Ellery Channing the younger, Thoreau's frequent companion and first biographer. The allusions to Europe in the opening paragraphs ("There's nothing like it [the beautiful sky] in old paintings, nothing like it in foreign lands,—unless when we were off the coast of Spain. That's a true Mediterranean sky.") refer to Channing's educational trip to Europe, sponsored through Emerson and his friends.

Thoreau then describes in detail the different animals and birds in his area: field mice who shared his hut; birds such as the phoebe, robin, partridge; red and black ants, whose ferocious battle he watched one afternoon near his woodpile. (As in the incident of the woodchuck, in "Higher Laws" this carnage awakens Thoreau's imagination; also, he recalls great authors of the past—Aeneas Sylvius and Olaus Magnus—who wrote of the battles of ants.) He also mentions cats, once domesticated, that course through the woods as if they were wild animals; there were the usual squirrels, raccoons, foxes, and woodchucks. Thoreau had also observed the loon in particular, accumulating quite a lot of knowledge of this bird's habits and enjoying its laugh or its dive for fish. He could also watch for hours the ducks on the pond, in fall days, "cunningly tack and veer and hold the middle of the pond, far from the sportsman."

CHAPTER XIII: HOUSE-WARMING

In October Thoreau began to get ready for winter, gathering grapes and different kinds of nuts, storing them away. It gave him great pleasure to watch, from September on, the changing landscape of fall turning into winter. He was now obliged to complete his house. Having studied masonry, he slowly and deliberately built his fireplace and chimney for two weeks with the help of a visiting poet. Although his house is of course more comfortable in the wintering air after it is plastered, he vows it never pleased his eye so afterward as when the air was able to pass through the cracks. His pleasure in his handiwork caused him to "dream of a larger and more populous house, standing in a golden age, of enduring materials, and without ginger-bread work, which shall still consist of only one room, a vast, rude, substantial, primitive hall, without ceiling or plastering, with bare rafters and purlins [beams] supporting a sort of lower heaven over one's head. . . ."

With freezing weather the pond began to form its first layer of ice. Thoreau observes how interesting is the first thin layer, where although it was only an inch thick he could stretch out his length and look through to the bottom of the pond in shallow places. Another sign of winter's setting in was the nightly flights of geese he detected. He also keeps a record of when the ponds freeze over. His chief occupation now is the gathering of firewood and kindling; he remarks on the affection a man has for a woodpile he has himself accumulated. He adds that during the second winter at Walden he used a small cooking stove instead of his open fireplace, but that "cooking was then, for the most part, no longer a poetic, but merely a chemic process." He felt as if he had lost a companion, because "you can always see a face in the fire. The laborer, looking into it at evening, purifies his thoughts of the dross and earthiness which they have accumulated during the day."

COMMENT

The gathering of firewood, and the "house-warming," may be regarded as symbolic activities: Thoreau was trying to maintain "a kind of summer in the midst of winter." In his little house, now shingled and plastered and warm, he had now "internalized" his life. He says, "I withdrew yet farther into my shell, and endeavored to keep a bright fire both within my house and breast." He finds, nevertheless, that the winter brings with it some estrangement from Nature.

CHAPTER XIV: FORMER INHABITANTS; AND WINTER VISITORS

As Thoreau winters at Walden, weathering several snowstorms, he is obliged to conjure up the past inhabitants of the woods. One of these was Cato Ingraham, a slave who had been permitted by his owner to live in his own house in Walden Woods. Cato had intended to use the lands for his old age but "a younger and whiter speculator got them at last." Both men have been dead now many years. Also, by the corner of Thoreau's field nearest to town, an old black woman named Zilpha had a little house where she spun linen for the townsfolk. She had a good and loud singing voice and made Walden Woods ring with her singing. Her house and possessions were burned during the War of 1812 by some British soldiers on parole. Down the road had lived Brister Freeman, a freed slave of Squire Cummings, and his wife Fenda, who told fortunes "yet pleasantly." Thoreau had seen Freeman's epitaph in Lincoln burying ground. The apple trees Brister planted were still growing, but their fruit, because untended, was sour. Other local inhabitants were the Stratton family, at the Breed's location, "a demon not distinctly named in old mythology, who has acted a prominent and astounding part in our New England life . . . New England—Rum." Thoreau recalls when Breed's hut burned, about a dozen years ago, having been set fire to by mischievous boys one election night. The latest inhabitant before Thoreau was Colonel Hugh Quiol, Irish veteran of the Napoleonic Wars. This intelligent and civilized man died shortly before Thoreau came to Walden. Thoreau remarks that, given his great curiosity about history, he would have made the colonel fight his battles all over again had he known him.

Thoreau had few visitors during the winter season. He merely lived "snug as a meadow mouse" in his hut, or took walks into the snowbound woods, making observations on the wildlife. His poet friend William Ellery Channing the younger came, however, "through deepest snows and most dismal tempests," as well as another "welcome visitor, who at one time came through the village, through snow and rain and darkness, till he saw my lamp through the trees, and shared with me some long winter evenings." This man—he was educational reformer Bronson Alcott, father of the novelist Louisa May Alcott—Thoreau calls "one of the last of the philosophers . . . the man of the most faith of any alive. His words and attitude always suppose a better state of things than other men are acquainted with, and he will be the last man to be disappointed as the ages revolve."

Thoreau mentions two other visitors. "There was one other with whom I had 'solid seasons,' long to be remembered, at his house in the village, and who looked in upon me from time to time; but I had no more for society there." He also expected the "visitor who never comes," he says: according to the ritual set forth in the Vishnu Purana he remained at eventide in his courtyard as long as it takes to milk a cow.

"I often performed this duty of hospitality, waited long enough to milk a whole herd of cows, but did not see the man approaching from the town."

COMMENT

The "one other" is probably Emerson. The ambiguous remark "but I had no more for society there," especially when compared to the longer, generous tributes to William Ellery Channing and Bronson Alcott, suggests the breakdown in friendship between Thoreau and Emerson.

CHAPTER XV: WINTER ANIMALS

After the ponds were fully frozen, they afforded Thoreau new and shorter routes to many points, as well as novel views of the same landscape. Sounds of the winter night included the hooting of owls, the honking of geese and especially the "whooping" of the ice on Walden Pond (similar to the cracking of the ground by frost). He could also hear the foxes ranging over the crusted snow, and in the morning the red squirrel awakened him by running over the roof and down the sides of his house. He fed the red squirrels and the rabbits unripened sweet corn, a meal shared by the chickadees and jays. When the ground was not quite covered with snow, or later when some of the snow had melted, he saw partridges feeding at the edge of the woods; often sportsmen would lie in wait for them nearby. Also on winter mornings sometimes Thoreau heard the hounds in chase, and the sound of a hunting horn proving that men accompanied in the rear. He relates several anecdotes passed on to him by hunters—for example, one Sam Nutting, a former bear hunter. It is interesting to note that the hunters used to exchange their skins for rum in Concord village. He also details how the squirrels and wild mice quarrel over his supply of nuts, or how a hare that lived underneath his house startled him by her departure each morning when he got up, with her thumping as she struck her head against the floorboards in hurrying away from the human above. He concludes by remarking, "What is a country without rabbits and partridges? They are among the most simple and indigenous animal products; ancient and venerable families known to antiquity as to modern times; of the very hue and substance of Nature, nearest to leaves and to the ground."

CHAPTER XVI: THE POND IN WINTER

Sometimes after a still winter night Thoreau awoke with the impression that a question had been put to him in his sleep: "what—how—when—where?" The sense of the question, however, is dispelled in "dawning Nature, in whom all creatures live, looking in at my broad windows with serene and satisfied face, and no question on *her* lips. I awoke to an answered question, to Nature and daylight." Then the glory of the new day sends him forth into his morning work. He went at the difficult task of getting water, for example: he had to cut through a foot of snow, then a foot of ice, before reaching water. Sometimes he fished through the hole in the ice, like the other fishermen who might come in the early morning, with reels and lunches. He pauses to comment on the rare beauty of the pickerel of Walden, with their colors "not green like the pines, nor gray like the stones, nor blue like the sky'" but of "flowers and precious stones, as if they were the pearls . . . of the Walden water."

In order to disprove to himself the rumor that Walden Pond was bottomless, he surveyed it with care in 1846; he did however find that the deepest part of the part of the pond was 102 feet, unusual for such a small body of water. The depth of Walden encourages him to philosophize, "What if all ponds were shallow? Would it not react on the minds of men? I am thankful that this pond was made deep and pure for a symbol. While men believe in the infinite some ponds will be thought to be bottomless." During the winter he surveyed and sounded the other ponds in the area, developing from this experience some theories on the structure of such bodies of water. Again he philosophizes that "what I have observed of the pond is no less true in ethics. It is the law of average. Such a rule of the two diameters not only guides us toward the sun in the system and the heart in man, but draws lines through the length and breadth of the aggregate of a man's particular daily behaviors and waves of life into his coves and inlets, and where they intersect will be the height or depth of his character. Perhaps we need only to know how his shores trend and his adjacent country or circumstances, to infer his depth and concealed bottom."

He describes how a hundred Irish workmen with Yankee overseers came from Cambridge to cut out ice from Walden. During 16 days they cut out large blocks of ice and stored them on the shore under layers of hay and boards. The total cut out during the whole winter was estimated to weigh 10,000 tons. Although some of it would melt during the spring and early summer, enough would remain to be shipped to warmer regions. Thoreau disliked the removal of the pond's "skin," but the ice had replaced itself within a month of completion of the job. He seems to like the idea that people of Charleston or New Orleans drink at his well, just as he himself bathes his intellect in Hindu philosophy every morning and feels that in going to his "well" for water he meets his fellows of Madras and Bombay and Calcutta: "The pure Walden water is mingled with the sacred water of the Ganges."

COMMENT

This chapter makes especially clear Thoreau's constant intellectual search for faith and the revelations he felt in the midst of Nature. For the question "what—how—when—where?" is answered by the living presence of Nature and its new dawn. (We recall the reiterated significance of each new morning to him.) It is an awareness of "life" in Nature that prepares him for the rebirth (of and in "Spring") of his spirit, a rebirth that is cyclic. Human nature is not shallow, he insists—and the analogy of deep ponds is further proof of our potential depth (the pond as a symbol of self): any analogy of humanity with Nature is to Thoreau a valid one, worth philosophizing about.

CHAPTER XVII: SPRING

Thoreau observed very closely the process of the breaking up of the ice and the gradual thaw of Walden and the ponds around, a process that he describes in detail, as occurring every day on a small scale. The ice cracks and booms with temperature changes; the ice begins to be honeycombed, and he can set his heel in it. With the melting of the ice and the warming air came the first plants above the now-bare ground, then the first birds. The phenomenon of the thaw fascinates Thoreau: "Ere long, not only on these banks, but on every hill and plain and in every hollow, the frost comes out of the ground like a dormant quadruped from its burrow, and seeks the sea with music, or migrates to other climes in clouds. Thaw with his gentle persuasion is more than Thor with his hammer." And at last spring seems instantaneous: "The change from storm and winter to serene and mild weather, from dark and sluggish hours to bright and elastic ones, is a memorable crisis which all things proclaim. It is seemingly instantaneous at last. Suddenly an influx of light filled my house, though the evening was at hand, and the clouds of winter still overhung it, and the eaves were dripping with sleety rain." In closing, Thoreau remarks that his second year, and spring, in Walden were much like the first. He left the pond on September 6, 1847.

COMMENT

Clearly Thoreau has made a metaphor of himself, his own inner purification and rebirth, out of the thaw, just as the entire episode of Spring is a reenacted myth of creation to him. (And we ought to note that this chapter contains some of his most poetically descriptive passages.) The symbolic ecstasy that Thoreau experiences

from the thaw, however, is a combination of his sponta-
neous experience of its actuality and his later reflections
on those two springs at Walden mingled with all the
other spring phenomena he has ever in his life observed.
Yet to him the coming of spring was no less than "the
creation of Cosmos out of Chaos and the realization of
the Golden Age" (thus he evokes, as always, the
ancients of the written word too). Through spring he
felt newly arisen as from a grave of winter (and deep
thought, mixed with sluggish discontent), "free in this
world, as birds in the air, disengaged from every kind of
chain."

CHAPTER XVIII: CONCLUSION

Thoreau justifies his withdrawal to Walden for two years,
beginning with "the universe is wider than our views of it."
Therefore, let us broaden our views of the universe. He says:
"I left the woods for as good a reason as I went there. Perhaps
it seemed to me that I had several more lives to live, and
could not spare any more time for that one." In short, he
found also that he could beat a path to his hut in the woods
as well as he could fall into a routine of existence in society
outside—or almost as well. In any case, life in the woods now
needed a freshened view contrasting it to life outside again.
His lessons learned at Walden were many and lasting, however. "I learned this, at least, by my experiment; that if one
advances confidently in the direction of his dreams, and
endeavors to live the life which he has imagined, he will meet
with a success unexpected in common hours. He will put
some things behind, will pass an invisible boundary; new,
universal, and more liberal laws will begin to establish them-
selves around and within him; or the old laws be expand-
ed . . . and he will live with the license of a higher order of
beings. In proportion as he simplifies his life, the laws of the
universe will appear less complex, and solitude will not be
solitude, nor poverty poverty, nor weakness weakness." What
Thoreau is really praising is the essence of his stay in the

woods, his own self-awareness. Thus he can say to others, "Explore your own higher latitudes." Furthermore, do not fear your own individuality, he seems to suggest in "why level downward to our dullest perception always, and praise that as common sense? The commonest sense is the sense of men asleep, which they express by snoring." (He is again returning to the idea of man awake, in all possible ways.) And "Why should we be in such desperate haste to succeed, and in such desperate enterprises? If a man does not keep pace with his companions, perhaps it is because he hears a different drummer. Let him step to the music which he hears. . . ."

Thoreau asserts that men need not "be shipwrecked on a vain reality"; that is, a man need not "turn his spring into summer. If the condition of things which we were made for is not yet, what were any reality which we can substitute?" He cites an illustrative anecdote of an artist who once lived in the ancient Indian city of Kouroo. This man desired to make a staff, deciding, "It shall be perfect in all respects, though I should do nothing else in my life." He worked on this task so long that time became unimportant, even though the city became a ruin and generations came and went by. His finished staff was indeed perfect, and he realized with some astonishment that "he had made a new system in making a staff, a world with full and fair proportions; in which, though the old cities and dynasties had passed away, fairer and more glorious ones had taken their places. And now he saw . . . that, for him and his work, the former lapse of time had been an illusion. . . . The material was pure, and his art was pure; how could the result be other than wonderful?"

COMMENT

We have here in the story of the Indian artist of Kouroo a parable of Thoreau's own work and, hence, his life. His writing, such as *Walden,* was much revised before publication; furthermore, his work was often enough ill received, requiring of him patience and faith in the individual worth of his "life-staff" in order to keep on working.

To Thoreau, perhaps the "staff" also represents "truth," whether of his work or his life, for he continues "Rather than love, than money, than fame, give me truth. I sat at a table where were rich food and wine in abundance, and obsequious attendance, but sincerity and truth were not; and I went away hungry. . . ." Although his generation offers philosophical societies, formally acclaimed great men, a lot of self-congratulation, where is there just one person who has lived "a whole human life?" To live this whole human life means to be as aware as possible, to admit life's novelty. "There is an incessant influx of novelty into the world, and yet we tolerate incredible dullness. . . . There are such words as joy and sorrow, but they are only the burden of a psalm, sung with a nasal twang, while we believe in the ordinary and mean. . . . The life in us is like the water in the river. It may rise this year higher than man has ever known it, and flood the parched uplands; even this may be the eventful year . . . ." The new dawn is up to the individual, however; for "only that day dawns to which we are awake."

COMMENT

It is clear that the waters of life rose higher in Thoreau than ever before during his stay at Walden. There he discovered, through simplifying his life, the novelty of the world, and particularly the world of Nature. It can be said that he went farthest toward fashioning that perfect "staff" of his work and his life during this period of voluntary withdrawal from the outside world. The fable of the beautiful bug (with which he closes) that came out of the egg in the dry leaf of an old applewood table is one of hope, of organic renewal. "Who knows what beautiful and winged life, whose egg has been buried for ages under many concentric layers of woodenness in the dead dry life of society, deposited at first in the alburnum of the green and living tree, which has been gradually converted into the semblance of its well-seasoned tomb . . . may unexpectedly come forth from amidst society's most trivial and handselled [shoddy] furniture, to enjoy its perfect summer life at last!" This is what the experience of Walden has meant to him, what he has attempted to describe in the symbolism of the deep pond (his inner self), the four seasons (the cycles of life, its stages), the thaw (reawakening), and especially spring (purification and rebirth).

CRITICAL COMMENTARY

As is true of most writers who have offered any sort of controversial material to the world, Thoreau, along with *Walden,* has met with a fluctuating critical appraisal over the years. In general, his contemporaries emphasized the doctrine of simplicity and the inherent romanticism in *Walden,* ignoring or misunderstanding its deeper philosophy and symbolism. In modern times, there has been a reevaluation of Thoreau, tending to focus on his complexities of thought.

THOREAU THE MAN

Thoreau was one of those "young men of fairest promise" whom Ralph Waldo Emerson addressed as they were graduating from Harvard in 1837. On this commencement occasion Emerson described such men, "who begin life upon our shores, inflated by the mountain winds, shined upon by all the stars of God," yet who "find the earth below not in unison with these," since they "are hindered from action by the disgust which the principles on which business is managed inspire. . . ." Apparently Thoreau took such words strictly to heart; he became, as Oliver Wendell Holmes later observed in what was the judgment of his own generation, a "nullifier of civilization." His biographers, such as Henry Seidel Canby and Carl Bode, tended to see him as essentially introverted; Canby, for example, called him a "dreamy child," one who "hated games, street parades and shows . . . company in the house," and "loved nature more than man." Even his contemporary and friend Emerson commented: "There was somewhat military in his nature not to be subdued, always manly and able, but rarely tender, as if he did not feel himself except in opposition. He . . . required a little sense of victory."

COMPLEXITY OF WALDEN

Thoreau's biographers infer a good deal from his major work, *Walden,* whose stylistic method and content seem to have been misunderstood by his earliest readers and critics. They considered his symbolism, for instance, extravagant "namby-pamby" or "stuff," and chose to read *Walden* in terms of its simplified, direct style. As for the content, these readers concentrated on Thoreau's act of withdrawal from society and, at best, read the book as social gospel that urged the individual to escape from corrupting civilization into the woods. These readers thus emphasized the romantic, escapist, back-to-Nature aspects of *Walden* at the expense of the larger philosophical, symbolic implications of the work. Modern critics, however, admit *Walden's* full complexity, granting it all the above-mentioned elements and more. They view it as a major work of social criticism of its time, in which Thoreau certainly was proclaiming against the stultifying influence of his American society on people's souls: these critics credit Thoreau with analyzing these degrading influences on humankind; with suggesting alternatives or solutions through his educational, cultural, and political theories; with strongly urging the substitution of selfhood—the search for the soul or inner nature—for racing after material wealth and power. As Sherman Paul points out, "To get men to see their universe symbolically, to read beyond its lessons of matter-of-fact, was one of the most liberating things Thoreau had to offer." "Not an escape, but the greatest discovery and gift," Paul goes on to say, was what Thoreau offered through the experience of *Walden.* In other words, Thoreau was trying to persuade us to reexamine our lives, to become more aware of our inner selves. *Walden,* then, which combines the record of Thoreau's experiment of living two years in the woods with his reflective view of this experience in the years afterward (from 1847 to 1854), relates essentially the author's personal struggle for purity, union with Nature, and selfhood in the midst of his own practical existence—in other words, Thoreau's spiritual autobiography.

THOREAU'S CONTEMPORARIES

James Russell Lowell was very different in personality and moral outlook from Thoreau, yet his review of Thoreau's

Letters to Various Persons, with general commentary, proved influential. Remarking (in the editorial "we") that he has currently been recollecting Thoreau's writings, Lowell attempts to give his impressions: "He seems to us to have been a man with so high a conceit of himself that he accepted without questioning, and insisted on our accepting, his defects and weaknesses of character as virtues and powers peculiar to himself. Was he [if he is] indolent, he finds none of the activities which attract or employ the rest of mankind worthy of him. Was he wanting in the qualities that make success, it is success that is contemptible, and not himself that lacks persistency and purpose. Was he poor, money was an unmixed evil." Lowell, in short, sees Thoreau as a prime rationalizer, as is further borne out in the remarks, "It is curious, considering what Thoreau afterwards became, that he was not by nature an observer. He only saw the things he looked for, and was less poet than naturalist." Robert Louis Stevenson made a more objective attempt to assess Thoreau, beginning with the assertion that "Thoreau's art was literature; and it was one of which he had conceived most ambitiously." He then discusses that "art," adding that "Thoreau's true subject was the pursuit of self-improvement combined with an unfriendly criticism of life as it goes on in our societies; it is there that he best displays the freshness and surprising trenchancy of his intellect; it is there that his style becomes plain and vigorous, and therefore, according to his own formula, ornamental." One of the most favorable comments on Thoreau, however, comes in an anonymous contemporary review from the *National Anti-Slavery Standard* of December 16, 1854. It is worth quoting at some length, since it captures the spirit of Thoreau's intent.

> These books [*A Week* and *Walden*] spring from a depth of thought which will not suffer them to be put by, and are written in a spirit in striking contrast with that which is uppermost in our time and country. Out of the heart of practical, hard-working, progressive New England come these Oriental utterances. The life exhibited in

them teaches us, much more impressively than any number of sermons could, that this Western activity of which
we are so proud, these material improvements, this commercial enterprise, this rapid accumulation of wealth,
even our external, associated philanthropic action, are
very easily overrated. . . . It is refreshing to find in these
books the sentiments of one man whose aim manifestly
is to live, and not to waste his time upon the externals
of living. Educated at Cambridge [Harvard], in the way
called liberal, he seems determined to make a liberal
life of it, and not to become the slave of any calling, for
the sake of earning a reputable livelihood or of being
regarded as a useful member of society. He evidently
considers it his first business to become more and more
a living, advancing soul, knowing that thus alone . . .
can he be, in any proper sense, useful to others. . . . The
fact of surpassing interest for us is the simple grandeur
of Mr. Thoreau's position—a position open to us all,
and of which this sympathy with Nature is but a single
result.

PRACTICAL VERSUS IMPRACTICAL

One approach to criticism of Thoreau is from the angle of
controversy over the practical versus the impractical Thoreau,
represented by critics Louis B. Salomon and Wade Thompson. Salomon evokes a "practical Thoreau" to counter eight
objections that he suggests students invariably bring up in
their studies of Thoreau; it is Thompson's task to prove that
these very objections raised by students are actually rather
sound, given Thoreau's expressed opinions—his conclusion
is that Thoreau is certainly inconsistent and that he is (as
Robert Louis Stevenson also suggested) an exaggerator. To
conclude thus, however, according to Thompson, is not
necessarily to be bound to dismiss Thoreau. The objections to
Thoreau are already familiar: (1) Thoreau thought he was better
than anybody else; (2) Thoreau didn't recognize the benefits
of commerce and machinery; (3) Thoreau was completely

opposed to organized society and government; (4) Thoreau thought people shouldn't do any work; (5) Thoreau thought all material comforts were bad influences; (6) Thoreau didn't recognize the practical side of life; (7) Thoreau was a hermit; and (8) Thoreau is trying to tell us how we should arrange our lives. In the case of each student objection, which Salomon has answered with refuting quotations from *Walden* and "Civil Disobedience," Thompson counters further with quotations that sustain the student objections! For example, that Thoreau "didn't recognize the benefits of commerce and machinery" is answered by Salomon with "I have always endeavored to acquire strict business habits; they are indispensable to every man." Thompson reminds the reader of Thoreau's statement "Trade curses everything it handles; and though you trade in messages from Heaven, the whole curse of trade attaches to the business." Or take the matter of material comforts as "bad influences": Salomon quotes, "My greatest skill has been to want but little. A lady once offered me a mat, but as I had no room to spare within the house, nor time to spare within or without to shake it, I declined it, preferring to wipe my feet on the sod before my door. It is best to avoid the beginning of evil." As Thompson ironically observes, "When a door-mat is evil, material comforts look pretty bad." As for Thompson's own countering quotation from *Walden,* Thompson cites, "I believe that water is the only drink for a wise man; wine is not so noble a liquor; and think of dashing the hopes of a morning with a cup of warm coffee, or of an evening with a dish of tea! . . . Such apparently slight causes destroyed Greece and Rome, and will destroy England and America." Asa matter of fact, both of the passages cited emphasize Thoreau's "exaggerated" asceticism. Such refutations and counter-refutations perhaps focus on the danger (and possibly inherent hilarity) of trying to find consistent ideology in poet-philosophers. Indeed, this is Wade Thompson's conclusion. "My main point is that Thoreau, on a literal residual level, is virtually amorphous. He is practical or impractical, prophet or blind man, naturalist or supernaturalist, 'a clammy prig' or a warm genial companion—depending almost totally on how one chooses to look at him. That students reject him for being impractical is—I hope I have demonstrated—only too understandable. In this respect I disagree with Mr. Salomon, who says: 'I hate to hear them [students] waste time arguing against him for things he not only didn't say but repeatedly and explicitly disavowed.' They are 'tilting at windmills that aren't even there.' The windmills are there all right; they are there in abundance—disavowals or no. These very windmills have been tilted at by men like Emerson and Stevenson and Lowell. . . ."

CONTEMPORARY VIEWS

Two contemporary views are of special interest: one draws a modern analogy to Thoreau's *Walden* and his philosophy; the other calls him "Christian in spite of himself." Wright Morris suggests that Thoreau shaped the natural grain of the Yankee mind, in a way that is still applicable, with his concept of Nature. The problem, according to Morris, is Nature versus Human Nature. He believes that "somewhere between Walden Pond and Boston—at some point of tension . . . the schizoid soul of the American is polarized. On the one hand we are builders of bridges and cities, we are makers of things and believers in the future. On the other we have a powerful, private urge to take to the woods, as we so often do." As further evidence of analogy between the time of *Walden* and now, regarding the problem of human existence, Morris quotes Thoreau: "I should not talk about myself so much if there were anybody else whom I knew as well. Unfortunately I am confined to this by the narrowness of my experience." According to Morris, "The revelation of this statement may lead us to overlook its accuracy. The narrowness of his experience is one of the essential facts in his book." The myth of Nature can be overwhelming, even traumatic. Thoreau turned to Nature and transformed what he found to suit the needs of his genius and temperament. He saw what he was compelled to see. "For all of the material details, the counting of nails

and beans, Walden Pond is a mythic, personal vision, and in
its depths lurk such facts as it is the genius of the beholder
to see."

Michael F. Moloney is concerned with Thoreau's "Christianity." Because of Thoreau's avowed pantheism (which sees
Nature as imbued with God) and his inherited Puritanism,
Walden is regarded as a search for spiritual certainty. To
Moloney this is a wrong emphasis, for Thoreau was still
involved in a form of Christianity and Christian principles. He
observes summarily that "Thoreau's passion for nature, his
reaction against the growing materialism of his day, his deep-
seated ethical, and less deep-seated but no less genuine,
religious concerns—these are the materials upon whose
intractability his creative imagination and his magnificent gift
for phrase sought to impose a final form." He admits that "the
problem of Thoreau's religion does not admit of easy solution. He early 'signed off' from the Christianity of his youth.
He did not go to church. At times he writes with what seems
calculated irreverence." Yet Moloney believes that "Thoreau's
negations, far from revealing an unsympathetic attitude, are
better considered as a clearing of ground for his statement of
affirmatives. No careful reader will doubt that he was a rever-
ent man." In fact, "At a time when Yankee ingenuity was
subduing the earth, and the gospel of success was proclaimed
from every street corner and town hall, he came to preach an
older and more abstemious doctrine. Intuitively, he seems to
have experienced the conviction that behind the Puritan
virtues of thrift and industry and provident concern with
material things lay the rather more than half-neglected truths
which gave these things meaning—truths which Puritanism
itself, in its best moments, remembered. In an age which was
rapidly reducing all values to one value and all standards to
one standard, and these not of the highest, he set himself in
the name of humanity against the tide. *Walden,* which
describes his relationship with his epoch is, ultimately a
humanist manifesto. . . . Man is Thoreau's primary concern,

not God. However, he was still near enough to the Christianity which he outwardly rejected to be quite certain that man
without the Spirit is not man." To this writer *Walden* becomes
a Christian humanist document.

The writer E. B. White, who also spent much of his life in the
country surrounded by Nature, recognizes the virtues, the vices,
the eccentricities of Thoreau, and he writes delightfully about
it all. He tends to bring together the issues and answer the
questions that have been raised above. White observes, for
example, that "Thoreau has probably been more wildly
misconstrued than any other person of comparable literary
stature. He got a reputation for being a naturalist, and he was
not much of a naturalist. He got a reputation for being a hermit, and he was no hermit. He was a writer, is what he was.
Many regarded him as a poseur. He was a poseur, all right,
but the pose was struck not for other people to study but for
him to study—a brave and ingenious device for a creative
person to adopt. He posed for himself and was both artist and
model, examining his own position in relation to nature and
society with the most patient and appreciative care. . . . Henry
was torn all his days between two awful pulls—the gnawing
desire to change life, and the equally troublesome desire to
live it. This is the explanation of his excursion." As White
goes on to say, what seemed "so wrong to him was less man's
economy than man's puny spirit and man's strained relationship with nature"—that is, Thoreau was not strictly a social
reformer. White observes, though, that to admire *Walden* to-
day "is something of an embarrassment, for the mass of men
have an indistinct notion that its author was a sort of Nature
Boy." Thus he raises and answers the question of Thoreau's
devotion to Nature. "If Thoreau had merely left us an account
of a man's life in the woods, or if he had simply retreated to
the woods and there recorded his complaints about society,
or even if he had contrived to include both records in one
essay, 'Walden' would probably not have lived a hundred
years. . . . Thoreau, very likely without knowing quite what

he was up to, took man's relation to nature and man's dilemma in society and man's capacity for elevating his spirit and he beat all these matters together, in a wild free interval of self justification and delight. . . . 'Walden' is one of the first of the vitamin-enriched American dishes." White considers it unfair to assess Thoreau's stay at the pond as escapism. "To set it down to escapism is, of course, to misconstrue what happened. Henry went forth to battle when he took to the woods, and 'Walden' is the report of a man torn by two powerful and opposing drives—the desire to enjoy the world . . . and the urge to set the world straight. One cannot join these two successfully, but sometimes, in rare cases, something good or even great results from the attempt of the tormented spirit to reconcile them." White concludes that Thoreau "was the subtlest humorist of the nineteenth century, a most religious man, and was awake every moment."

It can be said of *Walden,* then, that it clothes in deceptive simplicity (including style) its literary worth and philosophic depth.

ESSAY QUESTIONS AND ANSWERS

QUESTION
Describe briefly Thoreau's concept of Nature as seen in *Walden*.

ANSWER
Thoreau's view of Nature is essentially the American Transcendentalist view that (1) it is a benevolent force; (2) it is to be enjoyed and reverenced; (3) through Nature there is not only knowledge from the five senses but also intuitive knowledge; and (4) the ultimate goal is a feeling of communion or unity with Nature. For Thoreau the most direct line of communication was between the self and Nature. With this goal in view he developed his doctrine of simplicity; that is, he "went to the woods in order to live deliberately, to front only the essentials of life." In Nature, consequently, a person is nearest to God and godlikeness. He also felt it imperative to observe Nature's phenomena carefully, since there was a "correspondence" between every fact of Nature and human consciousness. Ideally, every physical fact of Nature could be absorbed into the mind; complete absorption resulted in the feeling of oneness with Nature, as well as a sense of liberation which, he hoped, could be passed on to others.

QUESTION
What is Thoreau's view of "civilized" society?

ANSWER
To Thoreau, civilized society is really a "barbarizing" element. In other words, the goals which the majority of civilized people subscribe to—material success, the work ethic, organized authority, general busyness—are barbarizing in the sense that they obscure from them their inner nature, that higher self to be searched for and found at the center of each person. Thoreau, for example, all his life detested the necessity for making a living, contending that it made his life "coarse." When first out of college, he resisted the pressures to join, as

a Harvard graduate, the ranks of clergy or lawyers or academics. He chose, at last, to wander as poet-philosopher, never really fulfilling the standards of the society of Massachusetts (and the whole of America) around him.

Also, he considered America and Massachusetts barbaric and brutal in the sense that their governments permitted and thus condoned slavery, and in foreign affairs, "overran unjustly" the territory of other countries such as Mexico. His position was that the individual, as part of a "wise minority" that might consist of just himself, had the right of conscience to challenge such governments. He spoke and wrote essays on this subject.

QUESTION

List a few details of Thoreau's actual life at Walden Pond, especially those that illustrate his "doctrine of simplicity."

ANSWER

In *Walden* Thoreau describes the test of a person's "inner necessities," which he seems to have applied both in fact and in theory; that is, he details the very physical environment he constructed for himself during the two years at Walden, and at the same time he suggests, in parallel manner, what are and are not necessities with respect to food, clothing, shelter. Thoreau lived as a vegetarian, for example; he did not even care for the fish he caught in Walden Pond, preferring the "cleaner" potatoes he might cook, and bread he might make for himself. Likewise, he dressed simply and functionally, and he observes how unfunctional much of our clothing is; he says it is designed to conform to the current fashion, which often has little eye for comfort or utility. As for shelter, he contended that our houses are in general too big, too wasteful, and too uncomfortable, as well as just plain ugly. His ideal for shelter was realized in the modest one-room hut he constructed by himself (except for a few weeks' help from a friend on the masonry), a house that was flexible with the seasons: in the summer he left it unplastered and open, so that the clean, fresh air passed through daily and he could feel the impact of mornings; in the winter, although insulated with plaster and a fireplace and shingles, he lived simply, cooking on his open fireplace (the second year brought a cookstove, which he found "unpoetic"). His own daily schedule was flexible according to the seasons, too, but essentially it was comprised of fulfilling the necessities such as procuring food, water, and firewood; reading and meditating in the morning and often the evening hours; walking in the woods and observing Nature; sometimes visiting friends in the village.

QUESTION
Describe briefly the use of symbolism and imagery in *Walden*.

ANSWER
The basic symbolism of *Walden* is of the seasons and of the pond; within these are the day, the dawn, the spring, the thaw, the reptilian imagery. Although the stay at Walden encompassed two years, in *Walden* he has condensed this time into one year and the four seasons that roughly parallel seasons of the mind and heart. (Winter, for instance, is a time of partial isolation from Nature, and of meditation, and somewhat of discontent.) Spring figures largely and exuberantly in the scheme, symbolizing purification and rebirth; here, and in other chapters, he signifies the blessed change from an old life to a fresher new life by the shedding of skin, by reptilian imagery. The thaw, too, is symbolic of this shedding of old life; and the entire phenomenon of the thaw was an exhilarating experience to Thoreau. The day also has its seasons like the year, and its essential one is dawn or morning, when, according to Thoreau, the mind is most alert: "Only that day dawns," he asserts, "to which we are fully awake."

BIBLIOGRAPHY

Anderson, Charles R. *Magic Circle of Walden*. New York, 1968.

Bloom, Harold, ed. *Henry David Thoreau*. New York: Chelsea House, 1987.

Boudreau, Gordon V. *The Roots of Walden and the Tree of Life*. Nashville, TN: Vanderbilt University Press, 1990.

Bridgman, Richard. *Dark Thoreau*. Lincoln: University of Nebraska Press, 1981.

Buell, Lawrence. *Literary Transcendentalism*. Ithaca: Cornell University Press, 1975.

Canby, Henry Seidel. *Thoreau*. Boston: Houghton Mifflin, 1939.

Cavell, Stanley. *The Senses of Walden*. San Francisco: North Point Press, 1981.

Channing, William Ellery. *Thoreau: The Poet-Naturalist*. New York: Biblio and Tannen, 1966 [1902].

Glick, Wendell, ed. *The Recognition of Henry David Thoreau*. Ann Arbor: University of Michigan Press, 1969.

Gozzi, Raymond, ed. *Thoreau's Psychology: Eight Essays*. Lanham, MD: University Press of America, 1983.

Harding, Walter. *Henry David Thoreau: A Profile*. New York: Hill and Wang, 1971.

_____, ed. *Thoreau: A Century of Criticism*. Dallas: Southern Methodist University Press, 1954.

Harding, Walter, George Brenner, and Paul A. Doyle, eds. *Henry David Thoreau: Studies and Commentaries.* Rutherford, NJ: Fairleigh Dickinson University Press, 1972.

Howarth, William. *The Book of Concord: Thoreau's Life as a Writer.* New York: Viking, 1982.

Lebeaux, Richard. *Young Man Thoreau.* Amherst: University of Massachusetts Press, 1977.

Myerson, Joel, ed. *Critical Essays on Henry David Thoreau's* Walden. Boston: G. K. Hall, 1988.

Paul, Sherman, ed. *Thoreau: A Collection of Critical Essays.* Englewood Cliffs, NJ: Prentice-Hall, 1962.

Richardson, Robert D., Jr. *Henry Thoreau: A Life of the Mind.* Berkeley: University of California Press, 1986.

Rutland, Richard, ed. *Twentieth-Century Interpretations of* Walden. Englewood Cliffs, NJ: Prentice-Hall, 1968.

Sanborn, F. B. *The Life of Henry David Thoreau.* Boston: Houghton Mifflin, 1917.

Schneider, Richard J. *Henry David Thoreau.* Boston: Twayne, 1987.

Seybold, Ethel. *Thoreau.* New Haven: Yale University Press, 1951.

Shanley, J. Lyndon. *The Making of Walden.* Chicago: University of Chicago Press, 1957.

Stevenson, Robert Louis. *Familiar Stories of Men and Books.* London, 1882.

Van Doren, Mark. *Henry David Thoreau.* Boston, 1961 [1916].

White, E. B. "Walden." *Yale Review,* autumn 1954.

Wagenknecht, Edward. *Henry David Thoreau: What Manner of Man?* Amherst: University of Massachusetts Press, 1981.